Sandy feet,
on the beach,

make prints in the sand.

Digging feet,
furry, friendly,

wet dog licks your hand.

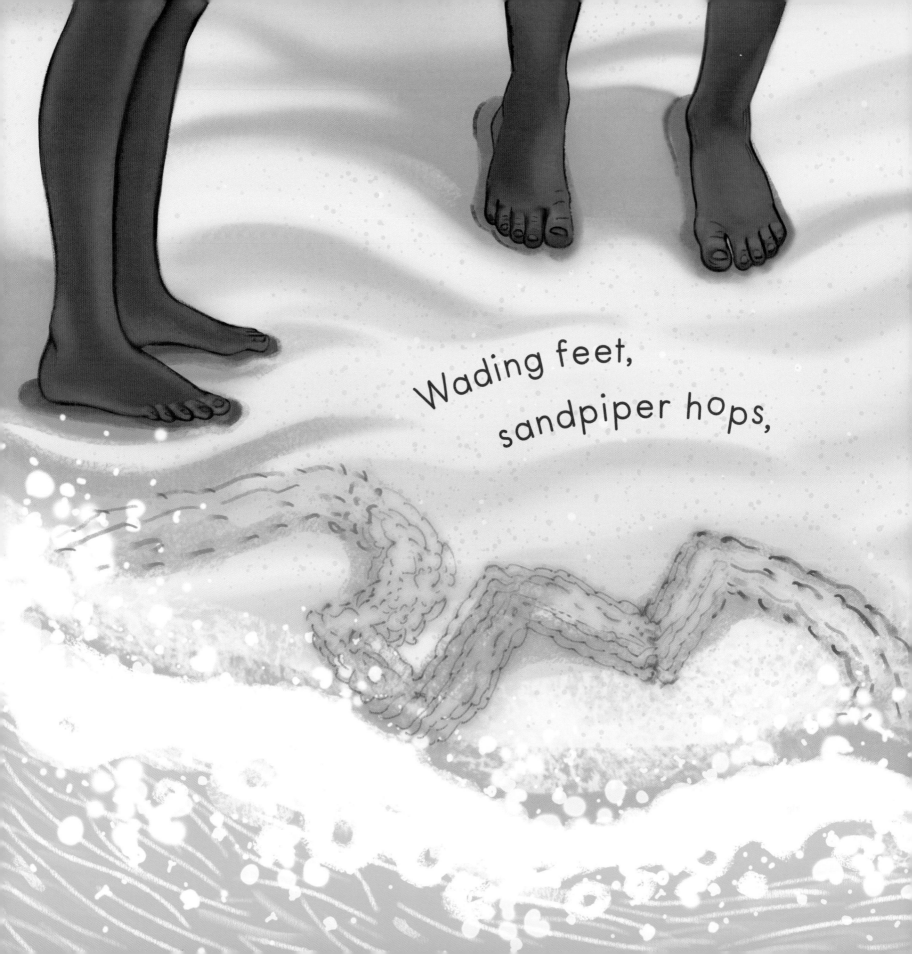

Wading feet,
sandpiper hops,

water curls
and sprays.

Crawling feet,
click-clack crab
scuttles on its way.

Stamping feet,
seagulls cry,
"Snacks for us to munch!"

Swimming feet,
webbed and strong,
pelican scoops up lunch.

Wriggling feet,
on five orange legs,

sea star makes its way.

Feathery feet,
barnacles hide
in shells of white and gray.

Scooping feet,
sea turtle works,
time to make her nest.

Running feet,
children play,

sand castles are the best.

Buried feet,
children laugh,

Daddy's toes poke through.

Tired feet,
sun goes down,

yawns, and eyes close too.

Sandy feet,
on the beach,

leave prints in the sand.

Whose Feet are Those?

Are you an ecology detective? Ecology is the study of relationships between living things and their surroundings. In almost every habitat—the natural home of an animal, plant, or organism—there are clues you can use to determine what kinds of creatures live there. Prints from "feet"—paws, claws, flippers, and more—are one kind of clue. Hunt for those prints the next time you're in a forest or near a marsh or by the ocean. Can you guess what creatures might live there? Why do you think they make that place their home, or habitat?

What prints can you find in your own habitat—your backyard, city park, or school playground? Take a camera or sketch pad and pencil with you to record what you find—just like a detective!

Here are the creatures whose prints we saw at the beach

Dog

The dogs we know as pets today came from wolves of long ago. Dogs have keen senses, especially smell and hearing, and strong instincts, or natural behaviors. Digging is one of a dog's instincts. Dogs dig to make a cool place to rest, to save a treat (like a bone) for later, or when they are bored. A dog's curved claws on its paws help it to dig.

Sandpiper

Sandpipers are small birds that wade in shallow surf with their stilt-like legs. They poke their slender bills into the sand to look for tiny crabs, worms, and insects to eat. When resting, they often stand or hop on one leg. These birds typically roam the shore in groups, so you may find more than one set of sandpiper prints at a time.

Crab

Crabs are animals with hard shells that burrow into the sand for protection from predators. Because of the structure and position of their legs, many crabs can only walk sideways. But a few species can move forward and backward as well. Two of a crab's ten legs have large pinching claws. Crabs use their claws to pick out bits of food from the sand and to protect themselves from enemies.

Seagull

Seagulls are birds found along the coast. They make nests at the shore out of grass and plant stems. As scavengers, seagulls feed on what they can find, but prefer fish, crabs, insects, and worms. To stir up small marine life to eat, these birds will stamp their feet in the sand, bringing food to the surface.

Pelican

Pelicans are enormous birds with giant bills and stretchy throat pouches. As they float on the water's surface, some pelicans use their huge beaks to scoop fish from the water. Others fly high above the ocean, then quickly plunge to pluck fish from the waves. With large webbed feet to propel them, pelicans are strong swimmers.

Sea Star

Sea stars—also known as starfish, though they aren't fish—move along the ocean floor using rows of tiny tube feet that cover the underside of their five arms. Each tube works like a leg—lifting up, swinging forward, and then planting itself in the sand again. Sea stars eat clams and mussels by gripping the mollusk's shells with their sticky tube feet and forcing them apart.

Barnacle

Barnacles are small shelled creatures related to crabs, lobster, and shrimp. They attach themselves headfirst to undersea surfaces like rocks, pilings, and buoys. Their scientific name, *Cirripedia*, means "feathery foot"; barnacles trap tiny food particles from the water with their feathery appendages, which they wave from their shells.

Sea Turtle

With their four mighty flippers, sea turtles are excellent swimmers and divers. In the water, they beat their front flippers like wings, and use their hind flippers to steer and balance. Most female sea turtles return to the beach where they were born to make a nest in the sand. They use their flippers like shovels to dig a hole, where they lay their eggs. When the babies hatch from the eggs, they dash together to the water.

You

What do you do at the shore? Do you wade in the surf like a sandpiper? Dig in the sand like a dog? Walk sideways like a crab? What kind of prints can you make?

For the passionate protectors of our beaches
—Susan

❧

To my beloved daughters, who make my life so beautiful
—Steliyana

ACKNOWLEDGMENTS

Susan Wood and Sleeping Bear Press thank Shannon L. Wells, PhD (Senior Lecturer, Ocean, Earth & Atmospheric Sciences, Old Dominion University), and Jamie M. Smith (Collections Manager, Mollusks, North Carolina State Museum of Natural Sciences) for their careful reading and review of the manuscript and art, and for offering insightful feedback.

Sleeping Bear Press™

2395 South Huron Parkway, Suite 200
Ann Arbor, MI 48104
www.sleepingbearpress.com

Printed and bound in the United States.

10 9 8 7 6 5 4 3 2 1

Library of Congress Cataloging-in-Publication Data

Names: Wood, Susan, 1965- author. | Doneva, Steliyana, illustrator.
Title: Sandy feet! whose feet? : footprints at the shore / written by Susan Wood ; illustrated by Steliyana Doneva.
Description: Ann Arbor, MI : Sleeping Bear Press, [2019] Identifiers: LCCN 2018037162 | ISBN 9781585364091 (hardcover)
Subjects: LCSH: Seashore ecology—Juvenile literature. | Footprints—Juvenile literature. | Beaches—Juvenile literature.
Classification: LCC QH541.5.S35 W64 2019 | DDC 577.69/9—dc23LC record available at https://lccn.loc.gov/2018037162

Photo credits pages 30-31: © Peter Kirillov/Shutterstock.com; © Mircea Costina/Shutterstock.com; © Jeff Skopin/Shutterstock.com; © Amy K. Mitchell/Shutterstock.com; © GlenroyBlanchette/Shutterstock.com; © aaltair/Shutterstock.com; © Belanger/Shutterstock.com; © Benjamin Albiach Galan/Shutterstock.com; © vlavetal/Shutterstock.com